The Light in the Valley

The people that sat in darkness saw a great light, and to them that sat in the region and shadow of death, to them did light spring up.

Matthew 4: 16 ASV

THE LIGHT

IN THE

VALLEY

A STORY OF FAITH AND COURAGE

PATRICIA NORMAN RACHAL
as told by Mary Boyter

NewCreationInspirations

Copyright © 2005 Patricia Norman Rachal
All rights reserved.

Edited by Patricia Norman Rachal

When I Met My Savior Copyright © 2004 Mary Boyter
Article "Miss Mary" Copyright © Caddo Parish Sheriff's Office. Originally published in CPSO newsletter, *In Pursuit*, Volume I, Issue I, Page 10-11. Used by permission.
Only One Hero Copyright © 1985 PNR
"God Helps You Live While Facing Disease", letter published in *The Times*, Shreveport, LA, March 31, 1999.
All Scripture from KJV unless otherwise noted.
Words of Wisdom from Living Psalms and Proverbs Copyright © 1967 Tyndale House Publications
All other Scriptures from e-Sword Version 7.1.0 Copyright © 2000-2004 Rick Meyers

TABLE OF CONTENTS

DEDICATION 1
FORWARD 2
PREFACE 3
REGARDING DR. JACK KEVORKIAN 5
NO ALIBI 8
A WORD FROM GOD 10
THE SHEPHERD AWAITS ME IN SHEPHERD'S PASTURE 11
THE ENTRANCE 12
BLESSINGS IN THE VALLEY 14
AS HARD VALLEY GETS DARKER THE LIGHT SHINES BRIGHTER 15
HOPE IN GOD AND GOD IN HOPE 18
BROKEN FOR A PURPOSE 20
LOU GEHRIG'S DISEASE IS NOT MINE 23
DARK SHADOWS OF ALS ECLIPSED BY THE LIGHT 26
SPIRITUAL BOOT CAMP 28
TRIO OF SUCCESS: PROMISE-COMMITMENT-FAITH 34
GOD'S DEPUTY–MIRACLES IN THE SHERIFF'S DEPARTMENT 39
GOD WORKS IN MYSTERIOUS WAYS AND PLACES 50
HE EVEN WORKS IN THE WATERMELON PATCH 53
A HOMETOWN HERO—ME? 55
HOW WILL I GET THERE? 57
BROKEN FOR GOD'S GLORY 59
MDA 60
LIFE ISN'T A PICNIC OR A BOWL OF CHERRIES 62

THE LORD IS MY REFUGE 63
MISS MARY 66
EPILOGUE 68

DEDICATION
By Mary Boyter

    I dedicate this book to several people. First, to my children, Beckie, Julie, and Joe. Without God's help and their care, I would not have made it for long.

    Second, to Dr. Robert Schwendimann and the MDA. In addition, to the many organizations that remain faithful to raise money for MDA, I thank you sincerely. Moreover, in particular, I wish to thank our courageous and hard-working firefighters. Every year they are out in the hot weather with their "collection boots." I had always donated even before realizing they were doing this for me—that I would have ALS (Lou Gehrig's disease). Research is important for ALS since there is currently no medically known cure. I pray everyone will be considerate and give when they see the firefighters out there working so hard to raise money for research. Remember that, as me, they could be collecting for you. Thank you to everyone who gives so generously.

    And, third, the Caddo Parish Sheriff's Office for hiring me. Thanks to Captain Sherrie Carter for having faith in me and seeing beyond my disability.

    I also give thanks to Dr. Frank and Mary Jobe. If it were not for them, I would not know Jesus today. When I went to work as Dr. Jobe's nurse in 1970, I had no idea how much my life would change. They invited me to church, and after making several excuses, I finally went. I gave all to the Lord, and Pastor Step Martin baptized me at Calvary Baptist Church. Last, this book would not have happened without the help of my friend, and author of *The Light in the Valley*, Pat Rachal. Much love and appreciation to each of you from Mary Boyter.

FORWARD
By Lieutenant Philip Escude', CPSO

People come and go throughout your life, but few make an inspirational impact on you as a person like Mary Boyter. Many times, we see people without knowing who they are or where they come from.

You see, as a person willing to work in clerical jobs at the Caddo Parish Sheriff's Office, Mary's duties of microfilming and filing seemed quite routine to us. Little did we realize when first meeting her that Mary suffered from Amyotrophic Lateral Sclerosis also known as ALS and Lou Gehrig's disease. ALS thickens the tissue in the motor tracks of the lateral columns and anterior horns of the spinal cord resulting in progressive muscle atrophy that starts in the limbs. Initially, to most of us, Mary was just another part-time employee who we were grateful to have because she was such a workhorse.

I had the privilege of working directly with her for a few years and can tell you that I never heard her gripe or complain of her duties or physical ailments. I never had to make a second request of a task I assigned her. Nor did I ever have to follow up behind her to see if a job had been done properly. On the few occasions Mary would call in because she could not come to work, I never asked why. I knew if she could not come to work she was hurting pretty badly or had some other good reason.

Many people give up on life faced with such challenges as a disease for which there is no cure. Not Mary Boyter; her attitude and desire amaze me. She is dependable, hard working and loyal. But more importantly is her faith in God that has enabled her to combat her ailments relentlessly in order to maintain such an active, productive life. Good luck and God bless, Mary.

Your admiring friend,
Lieutenant Philip Escude', Caddo Parish Sheriff's Office

Preface

The Light in the Valley is Mary Boyter's fascinating, personal story of living with ALS. With her courageous faith, she has continued to live a full and fulfilled life in spite of the diagnosis. Normal life expectancy is two years for an ALS victim. Mary was given one year when diagnosed sixteen years ago and is still going strong. She will tell you herself, it is none other than God's miraculous healing power. To meet Mary is to see the Light. I am honored that she has trusted me to pen her story as she told it.

I have heard Mary comment that people who know her know she is the same at work, church and home. She says of herself, "I am a what-you-see-is-what-you-get type of person. Am I perfect? No, indeed! I am human and make mistakes, then ask for forgiveness." As Mary's friend and the author of her incredible story, I know her personally and attest to the above as absolute truth. She puts up fronts or facades for no one. She is simply Mary, a woman of God.

If we are perfectly honest with ourselves, there is a bit of the skeptic in all of us. Skepticism arises within us about many things. Such as, what people say about themselves, proven facts (the true skeptic's mind is already thinking *proven facts?*), another's loyalty to us—the list is endless. But when someone says "God did this" or "God healed my body" or what about "It's a miracle!", then skepticism goes rampantly seeking some other answer.

I, myself, as a full-Gospel-entire-Bible-believing Christian have my moments of the skeptic eye's blurred vision. But there is absolutely not one thing in this entire world that could make me not believe that the Bible is completely God's Word or that the entire Gospel story as told in the Bible is irrefutably the truth.

Mary's story is entirely based on what God has done in her personal life and those around her. I have written the story as Mary has told it and believe all accounts given in this book with no doubt whatsoever that what she says God has done, God has done. There are few people in this world whose word I put that much stock in, but I can assure you Mary is one of those few.

If you have never had the privilege of meeting her, I hope you will someday. And if the coldest, hardest, most questioning skeptic meets her, I believe the warmth of Mary's heart will break that chilling ice of unbelief until it melts away. She is truly the kindest, most honest and patient person I have ever encountered, one who has an unwavering faith. I don't know anyone else I could say so beautifully portrays the character of Christ. Suffice it to say, in the words of Paul, "Whereof I was made a minister, according to the gift of the grace of God given unto me by the effectual working of his power. Unto me, who am less than the least of all saints, is this grace given, that I should preach among the Gentiles the unsearchable riches of Christ" describes Mary's purpose for living. She is truly a saint of God and one whose friendship and love I treasure. I have the utmost respect for this lady, Mary Boyter.

You will see that I am not the only one with admiration and respect for her. The article "Miss Mary" from *In Pursuit*, a magazine published by the Caddo Parish Sheriff's Office expresses Deputy Natalie Woodard's similar opinion of Mary.

REGARDING DR. JACK KEVORKIAN

My hope for this book is that it will serve as an encouragement to ALS patients. One thing I have learned is that we must find our purpose and set goals for our lives. In doing just that I have discovered there is quality life with this disease.

As I sit here looking back over the past fifteen years of living with ALS I am wholly convinced that I am a miracle. My finite mind will never understand why God has shown me such favor. But a wonderful truth from Jeremiah 29:11-13 tells me His thoughts toward me are peace and not evil, to give me a future and a hope. If I call upon Him and pray, He will listen to me. When I search for Him with all my heart and seek Him, I will find Him. These wonderful promises from the infinite God I know are a solid foundation for firm footing.

We must not continue to live in the past whether we have lost a loved one, have done something that shames us, or have a disability. The Bible teaches that there is a time for sorrow, grief and regret, but there also comes a time for rejoicing. Perhaps another way of saying it might be that when tragedy strikes and we fall apart, that is alright. But soon after, the time comes to pull it back together and get on with our life. When we continue in a state of depression and wallow in self-pity, it can block God from working in our lives. We must move on and put it all behind us. Until we do, our blessings will not come. God's Word says that if we have the faith of a mustard seed, we can move mountains (Matthew 17:20.) A mustard seed is very tiny so though the mountains loom largely, overshadowing everything else, it takes only a little faith to move into the positive light of His presence again. My praises are offered Him for my valleys because it is there that I grow and mature. God, with His power, fights my battles for me. (Psalm 24:8) He has all the power and has promised He will handle everything for me. In the words of an old hymn, "Where He leads, I will follow."

Webster's definition of faith is unquestioning belief, complete trust or reliance, loyalty, sincerity, honesty. The word faithful according to Webster is loyal, conscientious, accurate, exact. God is faithful. What more could we ask of Him? We must put our faith in His faithfulness.

God leads us by the Holy Spirit, which is how I knew He wanted me to start telling people what He has done for me. Speaking before groups was a legitimate concern because of the effect ALS has on my speech. I (unnecessarily) reminded God that Moses had Aaron to speak for him. He reminded me that I had been given more than Moses—that He had given me the Holy Spirit who would fill me and dwell within me. When we pray, if we just listen God will communicate with us through the Holy Spirit. He reminded me that Psalm 81:10 (Amplified Version) says, "I am the Lord your God, who brought you out of the land of Egypt. Open your mouth wide and I will fill it." Since then my motto has been "I believe larger with a spiritual charger." And, of course, God is the one who boosts my faith and charges me by filling me with His Word and His Spirit.

When one has a disability as ALS, a purpose and goals for your life are an absolute must. Even if you are not working, get out of bed and dress daily anyway. If possible, get out of the house every day and mingle with other people. Isolation is never the answer to anything, whether physical or emotional. Do not limit your contact to only disabled people. It is important to socialize with those who have no disabilities as well. **Believe in yourself.**

Sadly I have lost many friends to this horrible disease. I, the least of all people, do not question why it happens this way because I know some day God will tell me. I also know that no one has a right to say when a person's life ends, though he or she may be suffering from a horrible disease. Following is a letter I submitted to *The Times* in March of 1999 in response to an article about assisted suicide for an ALS patient:

God Helps You Live While Facing Disease
Mary Boyter—Shreveport

Re: Dr. Jack Kevorkian's recent assisted-suicide of a patient with Amyotrophic Lateral Sclerosis:

Our lives are not our own. We do not have the authority to decide when we have had enough or that we can no longer tolerate our conditions. God's Word states that He will not put on us more than we can handle. God does not cause bad things to happen to us. Neither I nor anyone else can explain why things happen, but let me tell you, He will go through it with you. Perhaps it will increase your faith in Him, making you a stronger person, but God does take bad situations and turn them into good. God is the only one who decides when your life is to end, and He doesn't need the help of Dr. Kevorkian.

The reason that I can make these statements is because I have ALS, or Lou Gehrig's disease. My symptoms first appeared in 1991. Not only have I had broken bones, but I needed a walker to walk with and had to use a wheelchair to shop. One thing that I have always believed is that God was going to heal me.

Today, I am walking and working part-time. Am I back to normal? No, my speech is not the best, and there are many things I cannot do. But I only concentrate on things that I can do and on loving life.

Believe me, I am the epitome of independence and have had to learn to ask for help. To me, that was the hardest part.

Yes, Lou Gehrig's disease is a hardship on families. But I want you to know that there is life with this horrible disease. If you want help, contact the local Muscular Dystrophy Association.

It is interesting to note that Ecc. 3:2 in the King James, American Standard, 1899 Douay-Rheims Bible and God's Word says "a time to be born and a time to die..." The Contemporary English Bible says "there is a time for birth and death..." and the Good News Bible says "He sets the time for birth and the time for death..." Suffice it to say God decides when our time is up.

No Alibi

People often ask of Christians, "How do you know you are a Christian?" Let me start by stating that I know in Whom I believe. The Bible says in Romans 10:10, "With the heart man believeth unto righteousness." I know I am a Christian because of the fellowship I have with Jesus. I feel His presence within me, an ever-conscious presence of the One that is the most precious to me. It is a delight to trust in His Word. I have kept His command to repent and be baptized. *"Except ye repent, ye shall all likewise perish."* (Luke 13:3)

I came to Jesus without excuses or trust in my own works. I didn't make promises or attempt to change myself, because I knew His changes from within my very soul were the only ones that would help me. Instead, I came offering no alibi but confessing I was lost—a sinner who had lost my way. I called on God to have mercy and save my soul. Turning from everything that was wrong in my heart and my life, I offered Jesus an empty temple to occupy. He would be the Captain of this ship from now on. I had come to want His will in my life. He cleansed me and I was born again just like Nicodemus in John 3:1-8. Jesus compared our new birth in Him to the wind when it blows. We hear it but cannot tell where it comes from or where it goes. So is the regenerated man; no one can explain where the new man came from or where the old one went. We see it but cannot explain it. We know it by faith.

Now, He dwells in this temple. I am a new creation in Christ Jesus, no longer conformed to this world but transformed by the renewing of my mind, with a new purpose for living and new goals in life. By His grace I am still walking in the newness of life, because old things passed away and all things became new. (II Corinthians 5:17)

Philippians 2:12 speaks of 'working out our own salvation' and that certainly does not exclude grace or faith in Jesus' atonement for our sins, for faith and works go hand in hand. I am not perfect so I have to work hard at staying focused on God and His plan for me, striving daily not to turn back to my old ways. Instead I press on with all my ransomed power working toward pleasing Jesus. I remind myself daily of how Jesus prayed for all His followers in John 17:16, "They are not of this world as I am not of this world." This world no longer has anything I desire to be attached to. I John 2:15 says to love not the world, neither the things that are in the world. If any man loves the world, the love of the Father is not in him. One of my greatest pleasures is spending time with other Christians. There is a special bond with others who also are in Christ. That is because our spirits will bear witness with His Spirit residing in other Christians. There are many in the world that deceive and say they are Christians or are 'born again' and they may fool us, but God knows His own so they won't fool Him. (See I John 4:1-7)

Second Corinthians 6:14 asks, "What communion does light have with darkness?" The answer is none, of course. God's Spirit bears witness with mine that He has translated me from the kingdom of darkness to His kingdom of light, as explained in Acts 26:18 and Colossians 1:13. I will not allow anything to come between my Savior and me.

A Christian is not known by his church membership or profession of faith alone, but as Matthew 7:20 says, it is by our fruits we are known. Or another way of saying that is simply that others will know I am a Christian by the way I live and give out of my innermost being.

As a Christian, one of God's children, my Father God rewards me (Matthew 6:1); disciplines me (John 15:2); listens to my prayers (Matthew 6:6); knows and meets my needs (Matthew 7:11); is merciful to me (Hebrews 2:17).

However long I remain on this earth, I will serve Him whose Light shines forevermore.

A Word From God

Some people say God works in mysterious ways, and so He does sometimes. But at other times He speaks to us so simply we understand exactly what He means. Perhaps even what may happen before the fact. *"Everything has happened just as I said it would; now I will announce what will happen next."* (God in Isaiah 42:9 CEV) Simple and clear was His way with me at a meeting in 1987. The crowd waited expectantly as the room grew as still and quiet as the calm before a storm. Brother Jesse, a seasoned speaker and evangelist, always drew a large number of believers and non believers as well with his humor and theatrics, if you will, used to communicate the Gospel effectively. Having never met him before, I was unaware of it at the time, but sudden silence was a bit out of character for his meetings. Nevertheless, you could hear a pin drop as he sought me out of the crowd and said God had a message for me. God's word was, *You will go through a hard valley, but God will go with you and will use you, and you will be a witness for Him.*

Brother Jesse did not know me or anything about my life. I was one face in millions he had spoken to through the years. But God knows every detail of my life, past, present and future. I am engraved on the palm of His hand. (Isaiah 49:16) I was humbled and thankful that God had stopped an anointed message and sought me out of the crowd to speak directly to me. God knows each of us so individually and intrinsically He knows how we will best deal with any adverse situation and equips us to do so. I knew in my heart it truly was a message from God, but the evidence was to come later—almost three years later.

THE SHEPHERD AWAITS ME IN SHEPHERD'S PASTURE

Do you ever feel utterly insignificant, like your life is going nowhere? If you've been there you can identify with how I was feeling early autumn of 1990. But my life was about to change forever when I went to a wonderful place called the Shepherd's Pasture in Jefferson, Texas. What a magnificent, peaceful place to pray! I could focus entirely on God and find out just what my life, according to Him, was all about.

After six days and in prayer every single morning I was beginning to feel a bit discouraged. I had not heard one thing from God. On Friday morning at 6:30 I simply asked Him, "God, are you there?" God was there and I soon knew it without a doubt. Much to my amazement my room began to fill with what I can only describe as a white cloud. For two solid hours I was simply glued to my chair. I had a life-changing experience with my Father God. The first part of that morning with Him I cried a river of tears. Then my spirit was filled with joy and laughter. Both laughter and tears are associated with healing in God's Word, so I obviously needed some healing. He alone knows the deepest recesses of my soul, the darkest parts of my heart even better than I know myself. As only He could do with His infinite mercy and wisdom, healing flowed through my inner being with love, comfort and much needed change resulting in sheer joy.

When I finally left the room three hours later with His earmark of dramatic changes within, my friends said I had a glow on my face and "Mary has been with God." How right they were. I had no doubt been with Him. His silhouette would forever be seen in my now (I knew) significant life. Soon after that experience, perhaps I was just stepping onto the threshold of the hard valley God had warned me about back in 1987.

The Entrance

When I went back to work, my eyes were blinded to the 'sign' blazing across the entrance: **Hard Valley**. I was on the threshold about to enter the place spoken of so long ago. Would I trust the One who had warned me of this very place? The door was opened wide, and I began my long journey by learning that I was being terminated from my job. Ironically this exit would be my entrance. Yes, I would trust Him without wavering.

I had arrived at work early every day so I could talk to Yvonne, a housekeeper, about Jesus. She was married to a strict, religious man who filled her head with deceitful lies. I knew numerous rules and regulations from any religion would not help her. Not only was Yvonne dealing with the confusion and bondage of a legalistic religion, her former lifestyle of prostitution and drugs had caused her to lose custody of her children. God said He would go with me through the valley, and already I could see the Light illuminating the way. Only Jesus could fill that emptiness so obvious in my saddened coworker, and soon she realized the void being filled with His love and grace. We rejoiced together as she believed in Him as her Savior.

Yvonne eventually left the company, and her husband, and went back to West Texas. She started attending church there and eventually started to teach a Sunday school class. In due time she was even able to regain custody of her children. The last time I heard from her, Yvonne expressed her gratefulness for my spending time with her to introduce her to Jesus, and I certainly have no regrets.

Even though I was not on company time when witnessing for Jesus, that was the reason I was terminated from the job. The company's specific choice of words, "Our policy and yours does not agree." At the entrance of Hard Valley God took my hand and I knew He would be with me all the way through. There would be no looking back. I had perfect peace in spite of losing my job. Reflecting back upon my time of unemployment I rejoice in God's faithfulness for He never failed to provide for me.

BLESSINGS IN THE VALLEY

Contrary to what one may think, being unemployed actually brought blessings with it. Now I had an opportunity to work with my church since nothing else was demanding of my time. The first blessing came when I was asked to help with the *Passion Play* making all the mountainous scenery. As I was making their mountains, God was moving mine.

Then another door of ministry blessing opened when I was invited to work with the singles' pastor, Brother David Sapp. Doors of opportunity continued to open as Sr. Pastor Allbritton and wife, Jean, asked me to help with Pastor's Sunday school class. Each Sunday morning I would arrive at 6:30 and cook breakfast for all the class members. What a blessing as the class was cultivated from about 40 students to a bursting-at-the-seams class of 100 plus students. There is always room for expansion in God's family so we weren't complaining.

Eventually I was among those chosen from the church to hold services in several nursing homes. As each new door flew open I made a joyful and fearless entry. I had the key—Jesus. I was not alone on this journey. There were six pastors and they all wanted me on their ministry team because they saw God's anointing on me. I am bragging on God, not myself. I knew that God was using me just as He had said. He blesses so abundantly, how could we ever repay Him? But repayment is not necessary. The debt was paid in full when God gave more than we could ever hope to give. For He gave it all—His Son, the Savior of the world He owns. (Psalm 24:1) And that makes us joint heirs with Him the moment we acknowledge Him as our Savior. I am now an heiress of all His blessings! As an heir we make no payments, but become forever grateful to the One who made us an heir.

As Hard Valley Gets Darker
the Light Shines Brighter

While on our Earth journey it is imperative that we follow God's leading. How? Listen to what He is saying to you—your heart, your spirit will know. And when you pray, you should not do all the talking. Remember, communication is two-way. Have some moments of silence in your prayer time and listen as God speaks to your spirit.

I am always thankful for God's intervention and never want to miss His leading. So simply following the path He had ordained for me led to a job in Dallas, Texas, in August 1991.

You have most likely heard the statement "you never know what a day may bring." God made the statement original in James 4:13-15, "You should know better than to say, "Today or tomorrow we will go to the city. We will do business there for a year and make a lot of money."What do you know about tomorrow? How can you be so sure about your life? It is nothing more than mist that appears for only a little while before it disappears. You should say, "If the Lord lets us live, we will do these things." (CEV) So peace with God is a very good thing. We need it each day for life, or for death—for whatever a day may bring. Since we do not know what that will be we can breathe a sigh of relief that God knows the end from the beginning.

One fateful day as I neared a busy Dallas street my goal was simply to get to the other side. Mission not accomplished, but God's would be. I stopped traffic that day as I went crashing to the concrete. My destination quickly changed from the other side of a busy street to a hospital emergency room swarming with activity.

I was ushered into Radiology where x-rays revealed a hairline fracture in the coccyx, but something else waved a red-flag alert to the doctor—a growth on the pelvic bone. Alarm prompted him to immediately refer me to another doctor who ordered more extensive testing. My first reaction to that news was to call in the warriors. My pastor and three others readily came to pray for me. I explained about my detour and what x-rays had revealed. After being anointed with oil and prayed for, my faith renewed, I was released with the understanding I was to follow up the next day with more x-rays.

With meticulous technology the additional pictures were taken the next day, the tech careful not to miss a single thing. As she examined them closely she glanced inquisitively at me before excusing herself for a consultation with the doctor. Not surprisingly, the follow-up report confirmed God's ever-faithful healing virtue. There was no growth to be seen. Coincidence? Mistaken radiology report the day before? No, this was God's power at work. I had a companion in this valley who would never leave me alone. There was an undeniable brightness lighting my way.

The devil always had his stupid little imps hiding in the dark crevices all along Hard Valley. The little troublemakers, ever ready to pounce and cause any number of complications, did not escape my astute spiritual vision. Seeing the shadows, I was not caught off guard because I know where there is a shadow there is light. Progressing through that valley with me was the brightest Light ever, no batteries required, and it will never power down. But when Satan lost his status in Heaven, he must have lost his senses too, because he never stopped to think that God was going to be glorified no matter what hurdles he threw my way. He repudiated the luminous Presence in the valley, but I realized it completely.

A year later on another sunny day, bright hot with heat, he reared his ugly head again. The splendor of such a lazy summer day had me deep in thoughts of sipping icy-cold pink lemonade while gazing at the bright yellow ball in the cerulean sky. But the hectic Dallas hotel's steady stream of busy people prevented my staying in my dreamy thoughts for long. Moving with the crowd I followed signs and arrows marking the way for speakers and guests. However, my destination was unexpectedly and abruptly rerouted from a hotel meeting room to yet another hospital emergency room as I slipped while going down some steps. Not to be caught off guard, I knew who was at the bottom of this ugly scheme.

I was seeing bright yellow alright, but not the blazing yellow ball I had daydreamed about. The brightness of 'stars' naturally dimmed my vision now since the damage this time included a minor concussion. Practically head-to-toe injuries also consisted of abrasions, contusions, and a hairline fracture to my right kneecap.

Although the doctor said I should be hospitalized overnight I, against his advice, asked to be released. I had been praying and I knew God had been listening. The hospital, though reluctant, agreed to release me. In spite of extensive injuries my faith was strong that God's faithfulness had not abated; healing would come. And true to His Word, God's healing touch allowed me to go to work the next day as if nothing had happened. As He spoke softly to my heart not to sue the hotel, I submitted without hesitation because when God speaks, I listen.

HOPE IN GOD AND GOD IN HOPE

The year's end brought more changes. In December I moved to Shreveport and found a warm and friendly church home at Hope Community Church. Now the name is significant enough, but only God knew how much I would come to depend on that exactly—hope in Him, and hope does not disappoint. The adversary was about to "trip me up" again. But there would be no faltering steps in my faith. As a matter of fact, he was about to take a hike himself because more problems from him only shifted my faith into forward. There was no turning back for me. Not at all; I was in step with God who was staying right alongside me all the way to the other side of the valley. And the devil was on the run because each footstep through Hard Valley only heightened my faith and trust in my Savior. I would leave footprints of faith for others to follow.

Yes, the adversary followed me right on to Shreveport and in August 1993, tried his hand at destroying me again. As a result of a fall at work, I damaged the rotor cup in my left shoulder. It was miserably painful. The orthopedic doctor wanted me to have surgery at once. Now surgery is fine when you need it and God does use surgeons in many situations, but I knew the Great Physician and was not going to consent to surgery as a first choice. After all He had been the attending Physician a few times already in the past and was truly the best with a much shorter recovery period. So off I went to the elders of my newly found church. Jerry and Sterling and some others prayed with me expecting only the best from God. And God did not disappoint us; He fully met our expectations. Within a week my arm was fine. Healed. Made whole by the Great Physician Himself. No surgery needed. Rejoicing was in order once again as the enemy had been defeated and we, in Jesus, had the victory.

Jerry would once again be instrumental in my journey

through the valley. His shield of faith would thwart the enemy's attempt to destroy me from an entirely different angle. Leaving my extremities alone this time, Satan tried another devious plot. The crisp, fall day seemed ordinary enough as the pleasant conversation ensued in the Optometrist's waiting room. Jerry and I had appointments with a mutual doctor on the same day. My name was called and I went in unsuspecting of the fiery dart about to inflict its painful sting. Glaucoma! This diagnosis gripped me with fear. But, no! Fear would not get an advantage. I wouldn't allow it! Departing from the office I quickly gave Jerry the grim news. Well, the devil's scheme was already marred, because when I told Jerry the negative report, he knew what to do and started praying.

The pharmacist filled the prescribed medication for my eyes. I made my way home fully intentional of following doctor's orders. But God had a different plan. The church had joined Jerry and me in the fight against Satan, and the faithful Healer would again undertake the task for me.

A scheduled check up one week later revealed no glaucoma. I never even broke the seal on the medication. Praise God that He is so faithful and true to His Word. He said by His stripes we were healed, and I am living proof. I was glad Jerry had been there to verify that the eye doctor had indeed found glaucoma by necessary testing on my previous visit. In spite of the gloomy report I had gotten on that day, because God intervened I would see the crisp red, amber, and golden hues of many future autumn days. The Light would continue to shine in Hard Valley and I would see Him shine. The evil warrior's dart had fallen to the ground, painless and powerless—defeated by God's prayer warriors.

BROKEN FOR A PURPOSE

Well, in spite of the devil's attempts on my life I made it to 1994! The summer months would find him in hot pursuit again though. Such a tumble I took this time not only got me in trouble, but x-rays at Willis-Knighton Medical Center revealed that I was in double trouble. My left ankle had a double fracture requiring surgery. Some of the swelling had to be alleviated before that could be done, so surgery was postponed until the next day.

After my ankle surgery, a flurry of activity ensued as nurses and attendants ushered me into ICU. Complications had arisen after surgery demanding extra care. In addition to breathing difficulties (*in Him...and breathe...*) my blood pressure dropped dangerously low to 80/40 (*we live...and have our being*). At our most critical moments somehow we can, even if somewhat capriciously, connect with His Word within us. Was I about to exit Hard Valley straight into my Father's arms? Was the difficult journey over?

Now I hope you are not thinking God took a vacation or forgot me. No, that will never happen. He was always there, ever faithful, holding my hand. As He and I together tirelessly continued through the treacherous valley, it became a valley of peace because I knew God had a plan. The elders and some others from my church came and prayed for me, and true to His nature God intervened. I was out of intensive care the very next morning. There is purpose in everything that happens in a Christian's life. Someone, conceivably you, needed to know that God is with us even in the valley of the shadow of death. Now you do know because He brought me back unscathed to tell you.

According to the doctor I would be off work for at least six months. But I was already back on my "faith feet" and refused to believe a negative report. I had not yet reached the other side of the valley and had some traveling to do. In spite of screws, pins and one plate in my ankle I was ready for physical therapy. The doctor sent a physical therapist with strict orders of "no weight on that foot." I was in PT a week ahead of time. Being in therapy a week ahead of schedule was right in sync with God's all-important timing; there was a divine appointment awaiting me, for He was ready to do some spiritual therapy. During my three days of therapy, God kept me busy witnessing about Him in that hospital—precisely what He had said back in the 1987 meeting. Although I was in a difficult place in my walk, (no pun intended) God was with me and using me to encourage others. It is well worth the trip—even on a crippled foot.

The nurses came one day for me on a particularly special mission. As I went with them, they explained that the precious little 80-year-old African-American lady, a retired school teacher and retired preacher's wife, had not walked from December to May. They knew she had a heart problem but had not yet resolved her lack of ability to walk all those months. She was sitting in the hall in her wheel chair waiting for me. After asking her if she knew Jesus as her Savior, confident that she did I took both of her hands in mine and prayed for her healing. God was faithful to hear us and only one day later a nurse brought her to physical therapy while I was there for mine. She got right up out of that wheel chair and walked over and hugged my neck. What a precious sight to behold! God had strengthened her and shown His great favor to her. My new-found friend also started therapy. What an awesome God I serve! His wonders never cease to amaze me. God had turned what the devil meant for evil into good.

Another nurse's patient was very depressed and had withdrawn from talking with anyone—family or friends. Her caring and concerned nurse told her about me and how faith in God helped me maintain a positive attitude. This sweet 40-year-old lady came to see me. We were left alone for about half an hour. We didn't pray together that day, but there was purpose in the visit. A level of trust had been established and she had somehow caught just a glimpse of the Light in the valley. So when she came back again the following day I prayed with her then. A portion of each of our remaining days in the hospital was spent visiting with each other—the radiant Light illuminating more each day. There was such a marked improvement in her condition it resulted in her going home the day before I did. God is so good!

As a matter of fact, God was glorified over and over because He used me in so many other ways while I was in the hospital fulfilling the prophecy from all those years ago. With God, there is no barrier of race, age or gender. After five days of hospitalization, I went home with two screws, eight pins and a plate in my ankle. One of the nurses who was so special to me had no children and wanted me to go live with her and her husband. However, independent lady that I am, I declined her generous offer of hospitality, but will always remember her and appreciate her kindness and warmth of heart.

I was warned that I would be off work for a minimum of three months (previously that was six months; God is an excellent healer), but with the help of a walker I went back to work in just three short weeks. The devil was still sitting back there, stunned, on that three-month prediction wondering where I had gone. Surely you know me well enough by now to know that I am not belittling the doctor or his expertise. But God may choose some other way of doing things than what we are accustomed to. I guess I knocked Satan off his feet when I was on a walker within three weeks after my release from the hospital. He cannot keep up with God!

Lou Gehrig's Disease is Not Mine

When my symptoms started to appear in 1991, I was diagnosed with M.S. (Multiple Sclerosis), but further testing in 1994 revealed the proper diagnosis of ALS (Amyotrophic Lateral Sclerosis). I had begun to have speech problems which the doctors figured to be a side effect of the anesthetic used during my ankle surgery. But that was to be proved wrong. The source was much more serious than anesthetic side effects. After seeing four different doctors whose diagnoses all agreed, Dr. Benjamin Nyugen, close to tears, told me I was terminal. "It's all right," I comforted him. "God will take care of me." He thought I was in denial which is quite a common reaction to such bleak news.

After leaving his office, my next stop was my church to pray. No, I was not in denial. I accepted the medical facts and had full confidence in my doctor, but I knew God would make a way where there is no way.

The New Year ushered in a walker and a wheelchair which I had to use when shopping. But my Lord ushered in more encouragement. I knew He wouldn't let me down as my medical expenses soared with medication cost alone at an astronomical $900 a month. Enrollment in MDA was a great blessing to say the least. How thankful I am that the association helped so tremendously with the expenses. I can personally testify that their funds are truly used to help the victims of muscular disease.

A respiratory specialist had now come into the picture. Dr. San Padero deemed this necessary as my breathing volume was only 47%; normal is, of course, 100%. Such a dangerously low volume prompted him to give my daughters, Julie and Becky, his personal pager number. It was at that time he broke the dismal news that I had only a one-year life expectancy.

In spite of all appearances, I had full assurance God had neither left me nor forsaken me and would complete the good work He had begun in me. I knew He was working undercover all the time, but by June of 1995, praise God, He began to surface and the evidence was seen. I was soon off the walker and sent the wheelchair back. I continued taking my prescribed medication. Although I knew that it was God doing the healing, faith and practical common sense need a proper balance. Therefore, I continued to do as my doctors advised, while trusting God for healing.

By the end of the year the neurologist, Dr. Galloway, confirmed what I already knew—that I was indeed getting better. Even my difficulty swallowing ceased. I was once again breathing without the aid of medicine and was referred back to Dr. San Padero who performed a breathing test which showed my volume to be back up to 67%. He just shook his head in wonderment and said, "I had you buried by now." Even though he was surprised, I did not share the sentiment. I knew God had been working on me. How humbled and thankful I felt for His marvelous works in my own life. We do not deserve God's favor, yet He bestows it upon us anyway. God's goodness and faithfulness will never come to an end. I have no explanation of why He loves me so; I just know He does.

My insurance would no longer cover the $900-a-month expense for medication, but rather than give up hope, I went to Hope. Now, my hope is in God alone, but my church just happened to be named Hope Community. I went there to find some prayer warriors. They were there, armed and ready. The following week I was notified that my insurance company would pay half of my medication cost and my place of employment would pay the other half through 1997. Although I'm very appreciative of both sources of aid, I know that my true source of provision comes from God. He said he would supply all my need according to His riches in glory. (Philippians 4:19) However, God often works through people if they will let Him.

Although occasionally we may wish we could see what our

future holds, God said, "Take no thought for the morrow." He knows the end from the beginning. When 1998 came around, my mind was clear and free from worry; God had not changed His faithfulness so I would not change my faith. Just as I expected, He took care of my every need. The National Organization of Rare Diseases generously agreed to pay for my medicine for one year. This was extraordinary enough, but I do not serve an ordinary God, so it was extended yet another year, through 1999!

Since 1995 my doctors have sent me to LSU Health Sciences Center in Shreveport, LA once a year for the student and resident doctors to study. They say I am unique to all other cases of ALS. The simple explanation is that I am not unique, but that I serve a unique God.

Dark Shadows of ALS Eclipsed by the Light

Perhaps you would like to know a little about ALS, also referred to as Lou Gehrig's disease, named after the acclaimed baseball player who died from the disease in 1941.

The effects vary in different people. Some have both upper and lower motor neuron interference while some people have only one or the other. But most, like me, have both. Motor neurons are nerve cells that send impulses to our muscles. So, basically, ALS interferes with those impulses from the nervous system "telling" our muscles what to do. But the great news is God can bypass that interference with life-changing power turning the impossibilities into possibilities.

ALS has acute symptoms and devastating effects, but God is with us in the valleys as well as on the mountain tops. No matter what stage of the disease a person is in, God is there. The Psalmist said even if we go to the uttermost part of the sea or make our bed in Hell, God is still there. Even the darkness fails to hide us from His presence, for the darkness and the light are both alike to Him. (Psalm 139:7-12) So no matter how dark the valley, no matter how obscure the light, be reassured His light will never go out.

Early symptoms vary and may include difficulty swallowing, choking, stumbling and falling, dropping things, inability to use parts of your body, or in some cases, the entire lower part of the body, and fatigue, which means rest is vitally important. Aspiration, accidental intake of food or liquids into the lungs, also may occur. When swallowing becomes difficult a feeding tube may be inserted. Lung volume (affecting your intake and exhalation of air) weakens and required oxygen must be administered. Kidney and bowel function desists. Speech becomes impaired and ultimately inhibited. At this point a computer device can be programmed to talk for the individual. Oh, how incredible that God has provided medical miracles of knowledge and modern technology! In His infinite wisdom, He really does have an answer for every hindrance along the path of life.

This disease is a horrible way to die and the caretakers need as much prayer and encouragement as the patient, especially in the latter stage. At that stage of ALS the patient becomes bedridden and unable to move, at which time a caretaker, usually family members, becomes a twenty-four-seven necessity. More than one is needed because of the physical and emotional stress of the deteriorating condition of the patient. But in spite of all the negative aspects of this arduous disease there is still hope.

The Bible refers to "Christ, the Hope within us." (I Timothy 1:1; Colossians 1:27) Only the divine power and guidance from God can give enough strength for the journey. The only way to have that is to establish and maintain communication with God through prayer and reading/meditation of His Word. Seek daily to know Him and to know His will for your life.

I must know that God is directing my life or I cannot make it through even one day. There has never been a time in history when Christians—even in the best of circumstances—needed to be more in touch with God than now. He wants our hearts to touch His through praise and thanksgiving. And if we have a true desire to be of service to Him, God will work through us empowering us to perform His deeds by following His commands, which incidentally, we receive through communication with Him. Even in the Dark Valley of ALS, I will not let the Light grow dim.

Spiritual Boot Camp

God gives various gifts and callings to the body of believers, His Church. One of those is healing. Satan loves confusion and uses this very gift of the Holy Spirit to confuse those in the church, as well as those outside. Simply put, the gift of healing means the believer who has the gift prays for someone in need and God, not the person, heals them. Laying on of hands is referred to because there is usually a point of contact made between the prayer and the sick person. Even in a practical sense when doctors, nurses or other caretakers apply their particular field of expertise to the sick, the human touch aids in the patient's healing. That sounds so clinical, but it is true that even patients who were near death or comatose who have recovered often say they believe the caring human touch, both physical and emotional, aided in their recovery.

When God places a call on our lives, He expects us to heed the call and use the spiritual gifts He has given us. God has given me the gift of healing, so I utilize it by praying for the sick or those with some other need. If I refuse to pray, that would be disobedience to God, quenching (or stopping) the Holy Spirit from doing what He desires to do. God rewards my obedience with His mighty and miraculous healing. I pray, He heals—that's how it works.

People sometimes have doubts about direct healing from God which is often referred to as *supernatural healing, because credit for the healing is frequently given to the person, not to God. This causes confusion; thus, skepticism may become justified, but confusion and skepticism still do not change the fact that God heals. (*not to be confused with the supernatural of the occult which is Satan's attempt at counterfeiting God's work, which also causes confusion)

Never take credit for what God does through you. Part of the reason for the calling on our lives is to illuminate Him. Let your light shine so it reflects back on Him. Always direct the glory toward Him. He has entrusted you with it.

But God may not always do things the way we think He should. However, the Bible says He is just and right in everything He does. (Deuteronomy 32:4) I learned quickly we cannot dictate to the Lord what He should do. God is not manipulated with our words, and we should never try to manipulate Him with His. God's thoughts are not ours, and with His infinite wisdom and grace, He knows how to handle each request we bring before Him. As we progress through boot camp we learn His ways and to cooperate with His plan rather than developing our own strategy, assuming we know how He will handle every situation. A good example of one's own strategy and pride ending in disaster and death is mentioned in Isaiah 14:12-24. We cannot run the show, but must instead be open to receive our Master's instructions, being fully confident in the master plan, the one that will work.

In the following pages, you will read the remarkable stories of some of the wonderful people I have been privileged to pray for. I regret not keeping a record of all those whom God has healed. In the beginning I thought I would only pray for people with Muscular Dystrophy, but soon realized He meant all sickness. All the glory and honor is God's and I will not claim ownership to something belonging to someone else. It is only by His power that healing comes. I am simply a vessel through whom He pours His blessings.

When God shows His magnificent works in people's lives, it blesses me with joy and assurance to see Him so faithful to His promises. Our God is still in the miracle business. He never quit; if He had your next breath would be impossible. Since I have had ALS God has allowed me to witness His healing power first hand. As I reflect on the marvelous works He has done I am filled with peace and contentment.

As you read the following accounts, it is my hope that you

will realize two things. First, the amazing works God will do. He is exactly the same now as He eternally has been and will forever be. No aspect of His holiness, mercy, miraculous power, or anything else about His character has changed. He is the same yesterday, today, and forever. (Hebrews 13:8)

And second, God's encouragement to those with disabilities that He wants to use you—perhaps more so than those who have none. And especially to the younger generation, let your youth work for you. There is a special group of people that only you can reach. Take what you do have and use it to climb to greater heights. But you must believe in yourself and have faith in God. Paul encouraged Timothy in his youth. "Do not let anyone look down on you because you are young, but be an example for the believers in your speech, your conduct, your love, faith and purity." (I Timothy 4:12, GNB)

I feel I am the least of all people, but the Lord chose me and encourages and directs me by the Holy Spirit to do His work and His will. God will not play favorites. He will do as much and more for you. No handicap or disadvantage can stand in the way when God has a job to do. Keep this in mind as you read these overwhelming accounts of only a few of the things I have seen Him do.

When I prayed for someone the first time with ALS, my faith-filled confident prayer was answered with the devastating blow of her death. As I went to God sobbing with confusion and discouragement I asked Him what I had done wrong. The Holy Spirit gently, but firmly, told me my calling was to pray, not to question the outcome. I have come to understand that although I did not see her body physically healed I know God met some need in her life when I prayed. Otherwise He would not have led me to pray for her. The first person I prayed for who received healing was having relentless back pain and anticipating surgery. Since my first experience had been rather disappointing, I suppose I was somewhat amazed as miraculous healing coursed through his body abrogating the need for surgery. Completely different outcomes but God was still in control of everything in both situations.

Jacob's Well is a local coffee house where everyone is welcome in an atmosphere of Christian love, warmth, encouragement, and friendly conversation over steaming mugs of coffee. The panorama of faces reveals a broad spectrum of emotions. Some bare lines of anxiety and stress while others, to the contrary, reveal the peaceful glow that only comes from God's presence. As I surveyed the sea of faces one evening, my gaze rested on one young couple who had a compelling effect on me. Their faces clearly portrayed shadows of discouragement and defeat. Perhaps hopelessness had overshadowed the rays of hope we all have, but lose sight of in the face of tribulation. Keeping our eyes on Jesus can help us avoid a "sinking Peter" experience. (Matthew 14:25-31)

I introduced myself to the young couple. Conversation flowed easily as we sipped our coffee together and became better acquainted. Soon they began pouring out their hearts revealing their cumbersome feelings. Both had lost their jobs (no problem understanding that one) and the family was now on Welfare. As I encouraged them and prayed with them the shadows of hopelessness began to fade from their faces. Soon they were smiling with the hope of God's promises. His Word can lift us out of despair as nothing else can.

Later, when I saw them again they were still smiling. God had gone to work and our prayer was answered with both being blessed with new jobs. They are no longer dependent on Welfare but are once again self-supportive. God met their material needs and gave their self esteem a much-needed boost as well. Our natural tendency is to overlook the truth that God's provision was there all the time. His tool was the Welfare system until they could get back on their feet. So remember to give thanks for all the ways God blesses us. Things may be so obvious we blunder through them in a spiritual tunnel of blindness, not seeing them as His blessings. Yes, He wants us to work and make our own living, but when hard times come He has established sources of help we often fail to recognize as His answer to our dilemma. A good example of that is MDA. It has been a source of help for many with muscular diseases.

"Is someone among you in trouble? He should pray. Is someone feeling good? He should sing songs of praise. Is someone among you ill? He should call for the elders of the congregation. They will pray for him and rub olive oil on him in the name of the Lord. The prayer offered with trust will heal the one who is ill—the Lord will restore his health; and if he has committed sins, he will be forgiven. Therefore, openly acknowledge your sins to one another, and pray for each other so that you may be healed. The prayer of a righteous person is powerful and effective." (James 5:13-16, JNT) With this word from God as my guide I knew when asked to pray for Paul, who had cancer, the final outcome would be entirely up to God. I have no power on my own to make anything happen, but I know that when we are obedient to God and do things as instructed by Him, we will see results. With this in mind, I began to pray for Paul.

As a friend of the family I sat with them through the tense hours at the hospital and prayed that God's peace would embrace them. God enveloped them in His cocoon of peace as the clock ticked away the minutes, each one seeming like sixty. God saw them through each agonizing moment until Paul's health was restored and his life preserved.

When friends suffer it is like a knife wound in our own heart. For two long years a dear friend of mine had suffered with ALS and was now in a nursing home. Before she died I prayed for her to be healed, but God had other plans for Nila. A gradual acceptance was beginning to grow deep within me of God's way of doing things—even when the outcome was disappointing to me. Just because a person's healing is not obvious to our terrestrial eyes is not an indication that they never got healed. When a person passes from this earth to Heaven their bodies become perfectly whole. There will be no sickness, pain, or crying in heaven according to Revelation 21:4. The gradual acceptance has finally found its place of rest in my spirit. I can now rejoice that Nila is in a perfect body in a perfect place with a perfect Healer—God's solution His way.

Although boot camp is a "tough row to hoe," we learn some valuable life lessons in our training. Just as the military, we learn to fight and win our battles. Soldiers are trained in strategic warfare and combat, submission, loyalty and unity. We become experienced in spiritual warfare and begin to understand how to combat our enemy. Submission to God and loyalty to Him and to each other becomes the governing force in our lives. Our faith grows as we defeat Satan's strategy with our unwavering faith in God as Lord of all. Our trust in Him deepens as we experience His faithfulness. Soldiers have weapons to win their battles. God has equipped His soldiers no less effectively. The Bible is our Sword to wield against the enemy; our righteousness in God is our breastplate to protect us from heart-rending attacks of the enemy; our footwear is the Gospel of peace enabling us to tread on scorpions and serpents; the belt around our waist is Truth rendering us effective over all Satan's lies; our shield is our faith giving us overall protection from all harm. We are equipped to use our training just as a soldier; remember we are in the army of God. We can now stand in the enemy's presence undefeated.

TRIO OF SUCCESS: PROMISE-COMMITMENT-FAITH

Through the years an understanding has settled deep in my soul that God's promises and faithfulness exuberates my commitment and faith in Him. They complement each other. Here is how it works. We must believe (have *faith* in) God's Word, His *promises*. *Commitment* of our self and our time to God is also vital. Ask the Holy Spirit for leadership and guidance. Strive for excellence letting all you do glorify our Father. Let Him have first place in your heart and everything else will fall into its proper place. Accept His destiny for you and believe (have *faith*) that you are in His perfect will. Be thankful for those He brings into your life. Pray for them to receive healing and peace. Encourage them with God's Word and your testimony of what He is doing in your own life. When you pray, pray in Jesus' Name. Have faith that He hears you and will answer. Having *faith* in God's *promises* helps us stay *committed*.

Why does the *promise-commitment-faith* trio bring success? The words are filled with meaning that go hand in hand and have the dynamics that work mightily together. Notice that some of their meanings are even interchangeable.

Promise
Assure
Pledge
Guarantee
Something said
Divine assurance
Self-committal
Declaration
Be assured of

> **For all the promises of God in Him are yea and in Him amen unto the glory of God by us.**
> **2 Corinthians 1:20**

Commitment
Promise
Pledge
Vow
Obligation
Dedication
Loyalty

Faith
Trust
Confidence
Patience
Assurance
Loyalty
Belief/conviction

> It is better that you should not vow, than that you should vow and not pay
> Ecclesiastes 5:5 MKJV

> So then faith comes by hearing and hearing by the Word of God.
> Romans 10:17

To learn God's truth, we must search His Word. Indeed, *"what a wonderful world"* would become everyone's melody if we would all live according to His Word. Without it and the Holy Spirit we will not have the vibrant force of the successful trio in our lives. There will be no fruit. Abraham, Moses, Noah and many more could not have done God's work without the dynamic force of this terrific trio in their lives. I will elaborate on *faith* more than the other two of the trio because *faith* enacts God's *promises*, and with this dynamic duo working for us, *commitment*, though requiring effort and discipline, almost comes naturally. Just look at some of the things the Bible says about this triplet of power-packed words.

Ephesians 2:8 Grace has saved us, but it is through *faith* we believe. It is a *gift of God.*

Romans 10:17 *Faith* comes by hearing the Word of God.

Hebrews 11:1 *Faith* is the *substance* of things hoped for; it is the *evidence* of things not seen. (Note: **Substance** is the essential significance of something spoken or written; an indispensable element; main or essential part. **Synonyms:** root; core; staple; soul. **Evidence** is something that serves as tangible verification. **Synonyms:** testimony; attestation; confirmation; proof; testament; testimonial; witness (Webster)

2 Corinthians 5:7 *Faith*, not sight, is how we walk (or live).

Matthew 17:20 A small amount of *faith* (the size of a tiny mustard seed) can accomplish great things. We can move our mountains out of the way simply by speaking what we believe (have *faith* in) if it correlates with the Word of God.

Remember, without God's Word in us and our *faith* in Him we cannot produce what He wants us to in our families, relationships and personal lives. More importantly is the truth that when He returns, those of us who choose to have *faith* will have eternal life and go with Him. What does *faith* have to do with eternal life? What does faith have to do with our daily life?

Romans 3:23 We all sin and come short of God's glory. Therefore, we all must have *faith* in our Savior's atonement for our sin.

John 3:3 Each of us must be born again by believing (having *faith*) in the Gospel—that Jesus Christ died for our sins, that He was buried, and rose again.

Jeremiah 33:6 Our *faith* in Him brings us healing, health, abundant peace and security.

Isaiah 53:5 We are healed by His stripes. Healing is included in the salvation we have *faith* in.

Matthew 9:35 Jesus went about healing every sickness and disease among the people. Do you think *faith* was in their midst?

Jeremiah 17:14 When the Lord heals, we shall be healed—spiritually, physically and emotionally. But if we have no *faith* in that, shall we be healed?

God has certainly kept all the *promises* of His Word for me. I choose to believe (have *faith* in) this. Do you believe Him?

Some examples of His faithful promises follow.

1 Kings 8:56 Blessed be the LORD, that hath given rest unto his people Israel, according to all that he promised: there hath not failed one word of all his good *promises*, which he promised by the hand of Moses his servant. (note that he used Moses, a person just like us, in this endeavor)

Romans 4:13 For the *promise*, that he should be the heir of the world, was not to Abraham, or to his seed, through the law, but through the righteousness of *faith*.

Romans 4:20 He staggered not at the *promise* of God through unbelief; but was strong in *faith*, giving glory to God;

Ephesians 1:13 In whom ye also trusted, after that ye heard the word of truth, the gospel of your salvation: in whom also after that ye believed, ye were sealed with that Holy Spirit of *promise*.

Hebrews 6:17 Wherein God, willing more abundantly to show unto the heirs of *promise* the immutability of his counsel, confirmed it by an oath:

2 Peter 3:13 Nevertheless we, according to his *promise*, look for new heavens and a new earth, wherein dwelleth righteousness.

1 John 2:25 And this is the *promise* that he hath promised us, even eternal life.

I'm sure we will all agree it goes without saying that Jesus Himself is the epitome of *commitment*. Although He is indeed God, He still relied on God, His Father, while walking on this earth, just as you and I do. Read about His struggle (for you and me) in the garden of Gethsemane.

"And he was withdrawn from them about a stone's cast, and kneeled down, and prayed, Saying, Father, if thou be willing, remove this cup from me: nevertheless not my will, but thine, be done. And there appeared an angel unto him from heaven, strengthening him. And being in an agony he prayed more earnestly: and his sweat was as it were great drops of blood

falling down to the ground." (Luke 22:41-44)

It was that prayer that made it possible for Him to suffer the crucifixion for us so we could go free. No other explanation is needed for *commitment*. Can we follow His example?

You will see this pattern of *faith, promise,* and *commitment* interlaced throughout God's Word.

GOD'S DEPUTY—MIRACLES IN THE SHERIFF'S DEPARTMENT

Although I am now retired from the Caddo Parish Sheriff's Office, the years I worked there were fulfilling years filled with remarkable people and unforgettable experiences. My job started in September 1996 beginning in the Department of Identification and Records. As a part-time employee I was scheduled for 20 hours per week, but that eventually worked into 32 hours, and later full time. My workdays were Monday through Thursday. I would get up around 3:00 every morning and arrive at work at 4:00 a.m. or shortly after. On the clock time began at 5:30 a.m., but I would strive to get my work completed early so I could be available to help others. They couldn't keep me busy enough and wanted "another one like me." God sent me to Caddo Parish Sheriff Department on a mission. His life and empowering strength in me help me to complete every mission.

It is hard to be accepted for employment when you have a disability, but acceptance was not the motivating power in my life—God was. With ALS your muscles are affected while your brain is still fully functional, but the people in the department made me feel right at home, accepting me as a person and co-worker just as I am in spite of my limitations. My employment there allowed me to work in many specialized divisions. Fines & Bonds, Warrants, Organized Crimes Division, Criminal Investigation, and finally, the Caddo Parish Jail, all proved to me we are never too old to learn. I looked forward to going to work each day, ever thankful to God for enabling me to remain so active.

Let me assure you I am not in denial about having this disease. The changes in my body and the limitations that I have are every-day reminders. But I encounter joy and humor in the midst of my trials because of God and my relationship with Him. Some of those undeniable changes have already been mentioned like running and lifting, but there are also simple things you probably wouldn't even think of. Wearing dress shoes with heels is an impossibility. Or, for instance, if I sit on the floor I must have something to pull up on to get back to my feet. These are minor disadvantages though, and I will not dwell on them. As Paul, I do not lose heart. Even though our outward man is perishing, our inward man is renewed day by day. Our light affliction is but for a moment and works for us a far more exceeding and eternal weight of glory. (II Corinthians 4:16-18 paraphrased)

God and His plan for me are what I focus on so I will continue to look unto Jesus, the Author and Finisher of my faith. My desire is to please Him and do the work He has for me. If I had my way I would do His ministry work full time. One thing this lady has learned though is to be humble and content with the things I have been given.

Working with the sheriff's office brought many unforgettable acquaintances and new friends into my life. God's anointing on me to pray for my new friends and their families as He healed them is almost beyond belief. Memory fails to recall them all, but I will share some of their stories with you. My goal is not self-recognition but to avert others' attention to God and His will to do the same things, and more, for any one of you.

I will begin with one about new beginnings. Spring is brilliant and refreshing with all the trees and flowers beginning to bud and bloom, symbolizing the newness and hope of life. Vibrant hues of green and every color of the rainbow (typical of God's promise to Noah) remind us of the hope we have in God. Also, we are told in Genesis 8 that the dove returned, after being sent out the second time by Noah, with an olive leaf in her mouth to show that new beginnings awaited Noah and all those with him who had trusted God at His Word. Therefore, we often think of April as a time for new life and restoration because of all the signs of life it brings. We celebrate Easter in the Spring commemorating the death, burial and resurrection of Jesus

Christ as the Lord of life. This is the definitive representation of new life, new beginnings, for all who believe in His resurrection.

April of 1998, in one sense, was a new beginning for the Caddo Sheriff's Department. We moved to a new building, but before we moved in I asked Captain Sherrie Carter if Pastor could come and anoint the building prior to our moving into it. She very graciously allowed it. My pastor was unable to be there, but Dr. Hill from Blanchard First Baptist and Pastor Kendall Holley of Broadacres Baptist did come and anoint our new office. Many people have commented on the peace they experience while in our department. I know it is God's presence which brings the peace, because He is there bringing new life and hope.

One of the most miraculous things in our lives is our precious grandchildren. They touch the deepest places of our hearts in a very unique way. It is almost like experiencing motherhood all over again with double the love and joy but in a completely different way. So when a deputy friend asked me to pray for her troubled grandson I could easily identify with her grieved heart. My prayer closet was standing open with answers as I went beseeching God for peace and wisdom He alone could give. We knew as James says "our prayers had availed much" when this grandmother began to see undeniable changes in this child so close to her heart. God saw her bleeding heart and, because we prayed in faith, brought this boy into submission to Him.

Equally as precious are our own children, and when they are jeopardized we moms immediately declare war on the enemy and become strong prayer warriors. Such was the case of another deputy when her daughter became dependant on life support. Her family was called in only to hear that she had very little time left. Desperation in the voice on the other end of the line was apparent when I answered the 4:30 phone call at work that morning. Driving to the hospital in the serenity and quiet of the predawn hour gave me a chance to begin quietly praying for a miracle, for that's what it would take.

Full of hope, I entered ICU only to see a lifeless form lying in that hospital bed who truly did not appear to have much hope. But with God there is always hope. As I began to pray for her, I made sure the family understood that the oil itself had no power, that I had no power myself, but what I was doing was Scriptural according to James 5:13-15. They needed to know there is hope and healing power in prayer.

Allow me to interrupt my story a moment to elaborate on prayer. It is simply communicating with God and is the vitality of our service. To communicate both parties must take an active part. Speak, listen, respond, though not necessarily in that order. What do we say to God? To begin with, Psalm 62:8 says to trust Him, pour out your heart to Him for He is a refuge to us. Some versions of the Bible say tell Him each of your concerns or all your troubles.

We must also remember to pray for wisdom and anointing for any ministry we are a part of. Jesus said to ask anything in His Name and He would do it because it would glorify the Father. The implication, of course, being that the request is in agreement with His Word.

Confession of our shortcomings and sinful ways as humans is part of our communication with Him that keeps the relationship alive within us. We should ask for His mercy and to keep our hearts humble. Listening for Him to speak to our spirit helps keep the two-way communication open. We must beseech Him to remove our iniquities and cleanse us from all sin. Only God can create in us a clean, pure heart and give us a desire and hunger for His Word.

Above all thank Him for His grace and mercy in allowing us the privilege to minister with Him. Give God all the glory, diverting attention from ourselves, projecting illumination upon Him. In other words, *move over, Mary (or whoever)*.

Pray for those who are out of fellowship with the Lord and may not have a communicative prayer relationship with Him. Ask the Holy Spirit to touch them in a way they can understand and respond to.

If not for prayer and walking through each day in agreement with the Lord, I would not be able to be of help anywhere. His grace and mercy make this walk possible. It is imperative, not optional, that we pray without ceasing as First Thessalonians 5:17 says. In simple dialect "keep a constant attitude of prayer." *The International Standard Version Bible* says, "Continually be prayerful." Without communication with the Father now, what will happen when He returns for His Church? We must know how to pray. Following are some Biblical concepts that have helped me with my prayer life.

Begin by praising Him. Psalm 100 tells us to shout for joy to the Lord and to worship Him with gladness and joyful songs; to know that the Lord is God who made us, that we are His people, the sheep of His pasture. He further encourages us to enter with thanksgiving, praise and thankfulness; to praise His Name. He is good and His love endures forever; His faithfulness through all generations.

Search your heart. Psalm 24:3-4 explains that it is he who has clean hands and a pure heart who may ascend the hill of the Lord and stand in His holy place; the one who does not worship idols and swear falsely.

Pray for all leadership. Romans 13:1 says that all authorities that exist have been established by God and are to be honored as such. I Timothy 2:1-2 says we are to pray for everyone, authorities first. This pleases God and will result in peace and tranquility in our lives.

Pray for pastors and spiritual leadership. Hebrews 13:17 says we should obey and submit to our spiritual leaders for they keep watch over us and are accountable for this responsibility. By praying and respecting them we can make their work joyful, not burdensome.

Pray for your church family. James 5:16 tells us to pray for one another so we will be healed in all aspects: body, mind, spirit.

Pray for revival. In Psalm 85:6 the Psalmist asked God to revive us so that we, His people, may rejoice in Him.

Pray for a harvest. Matthew 9:38 exhorts us to ask the Lord to send out workers into the harvest. Souls need to be harvested (brought into His Kingdom). How will they know if no one goes to bring them in? How would we have known if someone had not told us?

Pray for your family members. In Job 1:5 we learn it was a regular custom for Job to pray for his family. Verse one tells us that Job was blameless and an upright man. He is quite an example to follow.

Pray for your friends. Job is again an example in 42:10 ff. After he prayed for his friends, God blessed Job more than ever before.

Pray for your enemies. Matthew 5:44 and Luke 6:35 say we should love our enemies and pray for them. God rewards those who obey His commandments.

Pray for your personal needs. Hebrew 4:16 so wonderfully encourages us that we can approach His throne of grace with confidence so that we receive mercy and find grace in our time of need.

Some examples of personal prayer requests follow: Healing (Isaiah 19:22; 57:18, 19); Mental and physical opposition (Hebrews 12:2-3; 2 Timothy 1:7); Root of sickness (e.g. sin, genetic, lifestyle); Praise and thanksgiving to God in all things. (Psalm 150:6; I Thessalonians 5:17-18); Finally, finish with faith. (James 1:6)

These are but a few examples gleaned from God's own Word. Throughout the Bible you will find so many more. Pray in a way that makes you feel at peace with God. He will listen to the smallest prayer but expects us to grow and will help us to mature in our prayer life. No prayer request is too small or large for our Lord.

Our dependence is entirely on Him, not on the things of this world. Jesus shows me every day of my life how blessed I am. He provides food, clothing and transportation. Without Him we could not take another breath. Acts 17:28 says it is in Him we live and move and have our being. According to that Scripture our very existence depends on God—every breath, every movement.

So what happened to the lifeless form in the hospital bed? After praying for their precious daughter, I spent some time with the family and then went back to work. Around 11:00 a.m. the sing-song beeps of the anticipated phone call finally came. I jerked the receiver expectantly to my ear. The words came like electricity through the air. Life support had been removed and she was conscious and alert. Joy flooded my soul because God had given this beloved daughter back to her family. How I rejoiced, giving God praise and thanks for, as always, being faithful to His Word and for using me as His vessel to flow through. Why me? I have no answer, but I am honored. The Bible says God heals. That includes every disease, even those that are yet undiscovered. A new name for a virus or bacteria does not render God powerless. He does not have to prove His case. Yet, out of His mercy for us, He has, by showing the evidence many times over. I beseech you not to be among those who are victims of deceit as Satan whispers his lies that are contrary to God's own Word in your ear.

Getting back to miraculous events, one of our deputies lay comatose in a hospital bed with potentially fatal pancreatitis. When his kidneys and liver shut down his survival rate was a meager 15%. But God had the other 85%. The family, desperate for a miracle, allowed my pastor and me to go in to him and pray. After many daily visits and prayers, gradual signs of recovery began to materialize. Amazingly, only a few months later he was able to return to work. Who but God could take the 85% negative and turn it into 100% positive, bringing our co-worker and friend from near death to return to work? Our God is indeed a powerful God!

One Friday evening around dusk I heard the familiar voice of my friend Zelda as I picked up my persistently ringing phone. Steve, the husband of a deputy had been rushed to the hospital after having a heart attack. The family had been informed by the doctor that with the blockage he had, Steve would be prepared immediately for open-heart surgery. With little more than an hour before he went in, his family members, anxious with the seriousness of his condition, asked that I start praying. The moment I started to pray, the Holy Spirit prompted me to go to the hospital to anoint Steve and pray for him there.

This time Zelda heard my familiar voice in her ear when she answered the ring of my call. "Could you take me to the hospital? I must pray for Steve there." She agreed to pick me up shortly. The automatic doors flung open as we stepped up to the entrance of the well known Willis-Knighton Medical Center. Stepping into the elevator we wondered if we had made it within the hour. The floors counted off, seeming an eternity, until we reached our destination. I looked around for a clock. 6:35! Just in the nick of time. We barely had time to pray for him before they wheeled him away to surgery. But the Healer was in the house. A detour to Radiology revealed an amazing miracle. I am sure they did a double take when x-rays revealed no blockages! God had worked miraculously and opened them all! He indeed is the Great Physician.

On a cool September morning before dawn it was my turn for a miracle. Still pacing the floor with pain and nausea at 3:00 a.m., exhaustion was taking its toll. The grueling pain in my back had been going on longer than I realized. Since I have a high tolerance for pain, usually by the time I feel the worst of it things are way out of hand. And this was definitely too much to handle so I phoned Zelda for help. Just before the blackness engulfed me, I was also able to make the 911 call as well.

The ambulance screamed to the hospital. The long hours of unrelenting pain had become so unbearable my blood pressure was now dangerously elevated. As the paramedics pushed through the emergency room doors, stretcher bound though I may be, I knew, even in my semi-conscious state, there were embers of the Light still glowing in Dark Valley. The doctor quickly ordered a CT scan which revealed a kidney stone. Would surgery be necessary? ALS had weakened my lungs so I couldn't be put to sleep, nor could I have a spinal anesthetic because of the disease's weakening effect on my muscles. Not sure what the outcome may be, a very concerned Zelda made some quick phone calls. Shortly after, another friend, Tess, arrived. Soon to follow were my daughters, Julie and Beckie, just as concerned.

Necessary paperwork and routine steps were taken before I was assigned a room. Although the doctor had hoped I would pass the stone, disappointingly the misty shadows of a Sunday dawn brought no relief. So he informed me surgery was the only alternative at this point. But I had not abandoned the hope of prayer. Surgery was not something I was looking forward to. Frankly, I was more afraid than I cared to admit. But with the Light still shining, though at the moment it seemed a little dim, I still knew a miracle could be just on the horizon. The anesthesiologist arrived and encouragingly said he would "breathe for me." In my present dilemma that was small comfort though. However, the surgical staff would have to be called in so that gave me a little more time to work with before the feared event. Prayer was my only comfort now. Preparatory events were clicking rapidly and smoothly along. Too rapidly.

Surgical nurses were on their way down the hall for me.

Taking into consideration that God had rolled away the huge boulder from the empty tomb Jesus had lain in, I knew He could remove a tiny kidney stone. Only a few moments from the dreaded OR I asked the attending nurse for one more attempt at letting nature takes its course to remove the stone. Miraculously, it worked! Excitement and joy filled the room as the nurses, doctors, and everyone in that room realized that we serve an on-time God who is never late. He never counts minutes and hours the way we do. He transcends time, therefore, is always just on time—even when it is at the last possible moment.

One thing for sure is although I cannot remember them all, the people who were in need of a miracle will never forget that mysterious undertaking in their dismal circumstances, and having had that encounter with God will undeniably corroborate His miraculous power. There will always be situations when God gives hope where there is none, healing when medical science cannot, or turn the parched desert into a spring of living water bubbling new strength and hope into a weak and hopeless condition.

Many doctors do believe and immediately acknowledge God as the miracle worker. Others are skeptical while some will acknowledge there had to be some power beyond themselves that intervened but are not sure what that power was. A doctor's education and training takes many years of intense study and hard work. They are taught to diagnose the origin of our symptoms from a medical or scientific point of view and then prescribe the cure their intense training has taught them. So it is easy to understand why many doctors are often amazed and skeptical when they see miraculous healing they are unable to explain. This is not within the realm of educational facts they know to be true. But that is where faith comes in. There may be no explanation because God cannot be explained, only known by faith. That is why He sent His Son Jesus to dwell on the earth for a time just as human as you and I. So we can know the Son who transcends time and knowledge just as His Father. He is the exact replica of His Father.

Thank the Lord for educated doctors and their dedication in caring for us when we have life-altering health threats. My hat is certainly off to them. Advanced medicine and research organizations such as MDA are desperately needed in this chaotic and puzzling world we live in, but they do have limitations that God will never have. He always has the final say. How thankful we all should be that He does because there is so much hope in that truth.

God Works in Mysterious Ways and Places

Since my mouth is used to glorify God, it came as no surprise that the devil attacked it. One spring-like day just when you want to be enjoying the newness of life and breezy outdoors of a March day, I was much to the contrary not enjoying all too familiar hospital walls. LSU Health Sciences Center was admitting me with a not-so-ordinary disorder. Strangely, only one half of my tongue was swollen.

"Her condition is serious," the nurse warned my pastor and a Christian brother when they arrived at the emergency room. But I assured them there was no need to worry; God was in charge. My condition must have posed a pretty serious threat though because the doctors thought it best to admit me to the hospital, although the only available room was on the Psychiatric Floor. No complaints from me. I knew God had work to do there too.

The slight improvement in my condition was banished early that night when my tongue started to swell again. As the young doctor came to start my IV, he explained, "My job is to check on you every two hours and prepare a report to turn in tomorrow." The doctors were uncertain what was causing this bizarre condition of only one side of my tongue to swell, but since I was there and had another great opportunity for God to work, I took full advantage of it and talked to young Dr. Mark about the Bible and prayer. He excused himself to go get his instruments. While he was out, my dear friends, Larry and Kathy Johnson came in and prayed for me. How marvelous that God responded so quickly! By the time the doctor came back with his instruments the swelling had once again gone down. Since he had not shown much interest in God before, I was glad that he was there now to witness Him in action that hopefully might peak his interest in that realm as well.

Physician and visitors vacated the room leaving me and the

other patient alone. Moaning and restlessness coming from the other patient's bed revealed she was unmistakably in agony. Excruciating pain wracked her body as she tossed and turned trying to find comfort. Early morning surgery was scheduled, but would her endurance last through the long, painful hours of the night? She was in dire need of immediate relief from this awful pain. Nothing brought the stranger of relief to her bedside. But I had a Friend who could easily escort the resistant stranger in.

There was no alternative but to take my IV stand with me and pray for her. As IV and I made it over to her bedside I began to pray. She needed help and since I knew no details of her situation, I continued to pray quietly in the Spirit over her swollen abdomen. God knew exactly what she needed. In the dark hours of the night, the stranger had been ushered in by my Friend. And the dawn of a new day would shine bright with His presence.

Before daybreak the doctor came to get his very sick patient for preoperative procedures. To his utter amazement she was out of bed, showered and ready to go home! Although the diagnosis had been an obstruction, her hard, protruding stomach had softened and the swelling was gone. Yes, God had gone beyond pain relief and healed the source of that pain. With the doctor's confirmation of the healing, she was released that morning.

When her nephew came to see her into surgery, how surprised he was to hear this lady he had never seen before say, "God provided and took care of her." He was so thankful to take her home instead of ushering her into surgery. Quite a change of plans, wouldn't you say? The Great Physician had, not surprisingly, come through again for someone in need of a miracle. His surgery was quick and painless. No pain, no gain? Wrong! No pain, God healed.

A swollen tongue and an intestinal obstruction extraordinarily sent two patients to the Psyche ward of a hospital. There is no explanation of why God chose to work in this seemingly mysterious way. But the important thing is that because it happened this way several people were influenced for God's glory. There is a saying "Where there is mastery, there is no mystery." The Master had been there.

HE EVEN WORKS IN THE WATERMELON PATCH

God truly does work in amazing, mysterious places. His ways are only a mystery to us, not to Him. For instance, He may send us to do His work in places we would not anticipate as God's fallow ground waiting to be tilled. Such was my "watermelon encounter" at a grocery store. I may consider the store a place where I am likely to spend too much money but not a place to meet with God's destiny. And He often uses very ordinary things to accomplish His plans. He ordains the paths we tread, so why, I wonder, should it surprise me that everyday life is how and where He uses us.

So off I trod to the "watermelon patch" to discover that whenever, wherever God uses us should never come as a surprise. I maneuvered my car into the parking space and turned off the ignition. Walking toward the unfamiliar store I looked for the entrance and a shopping cart. *Lord, why would you want me to shop on unfamiliar "shopping ground?* I glanced around to get a general overview of the layout of the store and headed for the produce department. My mouth-watering craving for a watermelon took precedence over common sense for a few minutes. Stopping dead in my tracks I realized this posed a problem for me—I couldn't lift something as heavy as a watermelon! I would have to find an employee to help me. Hopefully there would be someone in the department to assist me.

Approaching the vivid colors of fruits and vegetables of every kind, I saw no clerk nearby who might be available to help me out. As I examined the luscious-looking melons I wondered if the other female produce inspector might be able to help. I asked, and, yes, she would! Mrs. Wilcox was glad to help me. I told her that I had ALS and as a result had difficulty lifting things. With watermelon midair tears spilled from her eyes and rolled over the hard, green rind of the melon. Why the tears? She explained as she set the round, green crisis connector into my cart, "My husband has ALS and has just been admitted to a nursing home. Would you visit him?"

Now, you're not thinking coincidence, are you? This encounter was planned by God. Of course I would visit him. God had a plan and I couldn't wait to see how it would come together. Mystery creates curiosity and He sure had mine up. This was definitely not happenstance.

Does His simplicity (although He is a God so majestic His ways are past finding out) amaze you as it does me? His uniquely simple way of leading me to unfamiliar shopping ground (my, how we love our comfort zones) and then using what one might consider one of the least of His creations—a watermelon—to me is so ridiculously simple, how could it be God? A grocery store and a watermelon bringing two ALS patients together, who otherwise would never have known each other, is almost as complex as it is simple. But then who ever thought a whale's belly would be a classroom for Jonah where he learned an invaluable lesson that would change an entire city? Have you ever just thought about that—a whale swallowed a man and then spit him back up, and it kept the town of Nineveh from being completely destroyed. Oh, the wonderful ways of God! Yes, God could indeed use a watermelon to connect two people in crisis.

Less than a year into his illness, the Lord took Mr. Wilcox to his Heavenly home. But as long as he was in the nursing home my consistent visits were filled with joy as I remembered each time the juicy red watermelon that bound our friendship together. Had I ignored God's leading into unfamiliar territory I would never have experienced the blessing of my delightful watermelon friends—or the best watermelon I've ever tasted! How delectable and exciting life becomes when we listen intently to our Heavenly Father and follow up with trust and obedience to Him.

A Hometown Hero—Me?

I would never think of myself as a hero, but several years ago I received a surprising, albeit flattering, invitation from a local TV station. "Hello," I greeted the invisible voice. Phone to my ear I heard the inquisitive voice reply, "Mrs. Boyter?" "Yes," I confirmed almost as inquisitively. The unfamiliar voice went on to say she was from a local TV station that regularly had a segment of their newscast entitled *Hometown Hero*. They wanted to know if I would consider being the subject of said segment. Hmm, a hero—me? I didn't think so, but I knew God was somehow involved in this. Not to mention that this was a pleasant stroke to my vanity as well, so I readily agreed to participate.

God knows the end from the beginning so it was not coincidental that I met Mr. and Mrs. Wood not long before, also via the telephone wire. She had phoned and told me her husband had ALS, confident that I would easily understand and identify with their health crisis. Mr. Wood's rapidly deteriorating condition was quite obvious from the first visit. Sadly he was gone in just a few months, and it was during the last few days of his life on earth the unfamiliar voice had extended the invitation to be their *Hometown Hero*.

The Woods and I had a common bond with our mutual faith in the Lord. It seemed only natural to invite him to appear on the show with me, so the honor was even further bestowed to make my TV debut with a real hero, Mr. Wood. It is my belief that God's plan for our lives continues until our last breath. What an honor to have shared those last few days with Mr. Wood and one that I will always treasure. I am sure he would agree that the real hero is neither himself nor me, but Jesus as the following poem depicts.

Only One Hero

My sole desire is to please You, Jesus, my Lord,
To live and walk in your holy Word.
Let your Holy Spirit flow through me,
That everything I do will honor Thee.
Never to bring shame or disgrace to your Name.
To live for You, not seeking fortune or fame.
Keeping my eyes only on You, Jesus, as I run this race,
My ultimate goal—to bring others to acknowledge your grace.
To be a mighty warrior, in battles strong,
Long-suffering and patient, never returning wrong for wrong.
To keep the shield of faith about me in One stronger than I
In this battle so fierce I must conquer, or others will die.
To give up this race for one fleeting moment will never do.
I must, I must conquer and win souls for You.
When those around me look and see the battles won,
If they see only You, it is then You will say, "Well done.
A job well done, my child, so faithful and true."
"But, oh, my Lord and Master, I owe it all to You.
When the battle raged fierce and long,
I looked up to You; I was never strong.
Victory in my life while on this earth I tread,
Was accomplished only because You live, and I was dead."
Though enemies assailed and were slain left and right,
Cut asunder and killed by the Sword while I fought the fight.
Still it is Christ who is the Hero, not I,
For I am dead. He ever liveth (in me), for real heroes never die.

How Will I Get There?

God truly goes to great lengths to bring the precise kind of encouragement to us at the exact time we need it. He is omnipresent, or everywhere all the time. He (obviously, from my own personal experience) has a message to people and will get the message to them however He needs to.

Unlike God, I am not omnipresent. So as willing as I am to be wherever He wants me, I am limited to one place at a time. But God always has a plan and wanted me in Washington, DC. Flying the friendly skies or zipping about the busy interstate was not His plan for me. No, my feet stayed firmly grounded in Shreveport soil where God planted me. I have yet to finish growing here. But God's plan was about to come together in a way only He could accomplish.

I happen to know one of God's servants whose name is George. He teaches Legal for Law Office in Washington, DC. I found out when I witnessed to George he is a Spirit-filled Christian. Concern clouded his face as he told me about his pastor who had been diagnosed with Multiple Sclerosis. I reiterated the ways God gives me courage to face each day and keeps me in a positive frame of mind. When all my surroundings seem bleak, I look to the Light of Jesus who always brightens the way no matter how dark it may appear.

George told me later that his pastor listened intently of how God helps me go through the trials of a similar disease. God knew there was something in my testimony that would bring comfort to my Washington brother's pastor, so He saw to it that the encouragement reached Him. Specific things that we go through are definitely not coincidence. II Corinthians 1:4 says it best, *"He comes alongside us when we go through hard times, and before you know it, he brings us alongside someone else who is going through hard times so that we can be there for that person just as God was there for us."* (MSG)

George is a busy man and has been called of God to work in some high places. He also works part-time for the Pentagon and teaches courses for law enforcement, but he has to be very careful of terms and expressions of his faith and is not allowed to talk overtly about God, Jesus, or the Lord in such clear-cut terms. So God leaves my feet firmly planted in Shreveport and takes my testimony of Him to Washington, DC, and all over the United States through common carrier—George. He testifies of Mary Boyter's faith and how it strengthens her in illness and potential trouble and that Mary's philosophy is "all faith, no stress." Those precious people will most likely never know Mary Boyter personally, but through mine and my Christian brother's testimony, perhaps they will know God personally and that is our goal. I am a well-traveled lady, yet never left home. Who could do that but God? As my brother testifies in every state of the wonders of our great God, I rejoice that he takes my testimony with him spreading the good news of Jesus Christ. No flight ticket needed.

BROKEN FOR GOD'S GLORY

It would seem quite obvious to me that the enemy would know by now that whatever stumbling block he throws in front of me will be kicked out of the way and God will get the glory for it. Why does Satan think God allows his hindrances in our lives? I'll answer that one for him. Because our Father is always looking out for us and enables us to overcome every hindrance of our number one enemy. Jesus Christ in us is that overcoming power and will always defeat Satan. Each battle we win strengthens our faith even more.

Well, in June of 1998, God was about to get more glory as I crashed to the floor of my apartment breaking my hand. God promised me He would heal it in six days and He did. God is not a man that He should lie. You just know in your spirit when God assures you of something. You don't think, you know. And when you have that "knowing" within you, nothing can convince you differently. When I asked the doctor for more x-rays because I knew God had healed me, he thought I was being quite foolish. He responded with, "Now, Mary, with your nursing background you know it takes six to eight weeks for a break like that to heal. It hasn't even been one week." Growing weary of my persistence, he finally agreed thinking I would see I was mistaken. Instead he was surprised to see that God, as He always does, fulfilled His promise.

His Word is all truth. Jesus Himself said, "I am the way, the truth, and the life." On the other hand, the devil is the father of all lies and everything he says is a lie. So I have the freedom of choice to believe God's truth or the devil's lies. In exercising that liberty, I choose to believe God. Satan has a strategy but not a clever one. His endeavors always bring glory to my Lord, yet he never stops trying to destroy me. "Well, duh, Devil, will you ever catch on to this?" Probably not, considering his history.

MDA

MDA has been my faithful friend throughout my illness. I am proud to be their spokesperson. When asked to compose a letter for the 1999 drive package, "yes" came without effort. I told them a letter from me would testify of God and glorify Him. Their positive response was all the motivation I needed to send my faith fingers flying across the page telling of the ways God has helped me through all my trials with ALS. The letter follows:

> Being an ALS patient, I can truly use the old saying, "I have seen that, done that and been through that." In other words, I do understand. Of course, if I had a choice, like everyone with ALS, certainly I prefer not to have it. I am the epitome of independence and that is the hardest part for me, to be incapable of doing all things for myself. I cannot climb to change a light bulb, walk on an uneven surface or lift heavy items. Let me tell you I don't think of things I can't do, but what I can do. But you know what, there is life even with this disease.
>
> In the year 1995 I was on a walker and trying to continue working. I even had to shop using a wheel chair. I resigned from my full-time job because I felt that I could not give them 100% job performance. Although the company wanted me to stay, but with fewer hours, I did not think it would be fair to the other employees so I left my job on August 2, 1996.
>
> I have been off my walker since May, 1996. Since September, 1996, I have been employed part-time, taking one day at a time and loving life.
>
> My medication consists of Amantadine and Rilutek, multi-vitamins and vitamin E. You should take your medication as God works through medicine and doctors, but that is only a temporary solution. I do not depend on it, only on God.

Kroger sponsored a MDA benefit in my name with local, district and regional managers for the association, September 4.

Wafting through the autumn breeziness was the enticing aroma of hamburgers sizzling on a grill. But what was even more appealing was that every dollar earned was a donation to MDA.

As a member of the Board of the Ark-La-Tex division, I must say it is an honor and joy to serve in that office, just as holding the position of President and Secretary was. Such was the honor of being recipient of prestigious awards from MDA (1998-2000), the simple words "thank you" seem far from adequate. There are no words to express appreciation for all that the association does for muscular disease victims.

Although my days are long, being allowed to work and able to remain active has helped me tremendously. The greatest pleasure I get from this life is God revitalizing me one day at a time to be in His service and to work with MDA. When I help raise money, it provides funding for research. I pray that if the Lord does tarry a cure for ALS will be found. I know that God will richly bless all those who give of their time or money.

LIFE ISN'T A PICNIC OR A BOWL OF CHERRIES

Even if life was a picnic there are always those little pests waiting to devour all the goodies and sting where it hurts. Oh, but they're so easily defeated—if you get them before they swarm. So I stay focused on the positive things I can do and keep the goodies. Once I allow my focus to be diverted to the negative things—those I no longer have the ability to do—the pests invade my territory. I stubbornly refuse to let that happen. Those pesky little critters will not go traipsing off with my joy. Resistance to the enemy sends him running. No, I'm not a Superwoman or a hero and do not claim to be, but I serve a super God and the Hero lives inside me. So although my life may not be a picnic, I can sure have one along the way and not worry about the sting of the enemy.

Do I claim my life is "just a bowl of cherries"? No, and it is for the best because cherries have their down side too. Though they are sweet and delicious, if you accidentally bite into the pit of the cherry and swallow it that sweetness can become bitterness, for you can get very sick from poisoning that comes from within the cherry pit. So even if my life was "a bowl of cherries" that too would have its own "pitfalls." So instead of making our lives a picnic or a bowl of cherries, God made them real with occasional troubles, but He always has the solution. Psalm 34:19 says, *"Many are the afflictions of the righteous; But Jehovah delivereth him out of them all."* (ASV)

The Lord is My Refuge

The initial onset of ALS caused me to have leg cramps, twitching (involuntary movement of) muscles, falling, breathing difficulty, and strangling. I have not had these symptoms since 1996. I continue to take Rilutek (50 mg) and Amantadine (100 mg), both twice a day. It is such a blessing to have this medicine to help with the symptoms I do have. Of course, God gets the glory first, then MDA and the medication.

Even on the medications I still have limitations. Some days I have more energy than others. There are some things beyond the scope of my ability. To say some of them are not missed would be untrue. For example running, bowling, jogging, and playing tennis are things I miss. Lacking the assistance of a rail, or another person, I can no longer climb stairs. Without hesitation, I will say I would rather be completely free of symptoms. But God has given me so much more I can do. He graciously allows me to live independently and serve Him. My walk with God is the most important part of my life.

I'm not out of Hard Valley yet, but as long as I am in the valley I will look toward the Light. This is not the end of my story, but I cannot end this without expressing my amazement at how the Lord works. To summarize, I will just say that I do not know if God will choose to completely heal me of ALS while I am on this earth, but whether He does or not I will continue to speak of His grace and mercy. The following quotes from God's Word epitomize God's acts in my life:

Job 9:10, "Which doeth great things past finding out; yea, and wonders without number."

Psalm 77:11, "I will remember the works of the Lord: surely I will remember thy wonders of old."

Psalm 77:14, "Thou art the God that doest wonders: thou hast declared thy strength among the people."

Psalm 89:5, "And the heavens shall praise thy wonders, O

Lord: thy faithfulness also in the congregation of the saints."

Psalm 96:3, "Declare his glory among the heathen, his wonders among all people."

Psalm 105:5, "Remember his marvelous works that he hath done; his wonders, and the judgments of his mouth."

Psalm 136:4, "To him who alone doeth great wonders: for his mercy endureth for ever."

I can truly reiterate the Psalmist's own words: *"Lord, You are my refuge! Don't let me down! Save me from my enemies, for You are just! Rescue me! Bend down Your ear and listen to my plea and save me. Be to me a great protecting rock, where I am always welcome, safe from all attacks. For You have issued the order to save me. Rescue me, O God, from these unjust and cruel men. O Lord, You alone are my hope; I've trusted You from childhood. Yes, You have been with me from birth and have helped me constantly—no wonder I am always praising You. My success—at which so many stand amazed—is because You are my mighty protector. All day long I'll praise and honor You, O God, for all that You have done for me. I would have despaired and perished unless Your laws had been my deepest delight. I will never lay aside Your laws, for you have used them to restore my joy and health. I am Yours! Save me! For I have tried to live according to Your desires. Though the wicked hide along the way to kill me, I will quietly keep my mind upon Your promises."* (Psalm 71:1-8; 119:92-95 TLB)

I encourage every ALS patient to stay active as long as possible and to make time for the Lord. Wherever you are in your walk, whether in a valley or on a mountain top, when Satan surrounds you in darkness remember to look up. The Light is still there though dim it may seem. Let His light shine through you in this dark world. If you do this, you will maintain an amazing peace and joy. One thing I know—when we know God and communicate with Him and walk according to His Word death actually means life. Someday I will exit Hard Valley straight into my Savior's arms, but until that time I will follow the advice of a faithful, trustworthy Friend who is with me everywhere I go. "Give your entire attention to what God is doing right now, and don't get worked up about what may or may not happen tomorrow. God will help you deal with whatever hard things come up when the time comes." (Jesus in Matthew 6:34, MSG) Jesus is the Light of my life. As long as He illuminates Hard Valley I can always find my way. There will come a time when I exit this dark valley straight into Heaven's gates. When that day comes I will forever praise the One whose brilliance is such that no other light is needed. I will forever look upon the face of the Everlasting Light that led me through the valley.

MISS MARY
By Deputy Natalie Woodard, CPSO

She is sincere, sweet and has the patience of a saint, an inspiration to many that know her and a firm believer in the work of the Lord. She is early to work, brightening the mornings of those who come in after her with her cheerful outlook and quick smile. We all know her as Miss Mary, the gentle, kind-eyed soul who listens intently when you speak and offers words of comfort and wisdom when our days aren't going quite as we'd like.

She first came to the Sheriff's Office four years ago, working part-time in the Identification Division, where I first came to know her. Upon first meeting her, you notice her sparkling eyes reflecting the smile upon her lips. Her soft voice is somewhat faltering and slow, but her intelligence and quick wit soon become evident. Nothing gets by her. She has seemingly boundless energy and offers so much of herself that she is a true inspiration.

Miss Mary suffers from Lou Gehrig's disease, a debilitating, often fatal, illness that strikes insidiously. Though the disease has taken its toll on Miss Mary, her enthusiasm and belief in the power of prayer have brought her to where she is today. Diagnosed in 1991 with the disease, Miss Mary frequently suffered broken bones, something she put off to clumsiness. However, when speech became difficult, she sought answers to what seemed to be just an annoying problem. Not letting the diagnosis impede her life, she turned herself over to the Lord, at first seeking answers, then accepting God's fate. She sees herself as being blessed and that it is her mission to give comfort to others with the same debilitating disease. She says, "God is doing this for me so that I can encourage others." Not, God has done this to me, but that he has done it for me—a perspective few of us could embrace.

Becoming a full time employee just over a year ago, she has refused to let the disease take over her life and shows up for work at Caddo Correctional Center where she works at the jail's visitation desk answering phones and doing computer work. Miss Mary is a very capable, dependable employee and is a pleasure to work with.

She is unstoppable in her quest to help others, volunteering herself to the Muscular Dystrophy Association, doing whatever she can. On Labor Day weekend, one can find her volunteering at the Jerry Lewis MDA Telethon giving her time, energy and zest for life. She is a tireless speaker at church and group functions, giving encouragement to those who have lost the will to continue in the face of disease. She cares for her mother who lives in a nearby nursing home and keeps contact with her children and grandchildren. She is an inspiration to all of us, a paragon of faith and a reminder that sometimes even when life has dealt us unfairness, it's all in what you do with what you have been given—hope is never lost. I would say Miss Mary is quite a rarity and that the Sheriff's Office has an exquisite treasure on their hands.

Lou Gehrig's is a progressive disease that attacks nerve cells in the brain and spinal cord. When nerve cells are attacked, the affected muscles waste away, causing degeneration and hardening in the area. As the disease progresses, total paralysis is often in the future. Speech may become affected as the disease destroys the muscles and nerves that control normal swallowing and breathing. Limbs look "thinner" as muscle tissue atrophies and walking may be impaired. Mental agility is not usually affected in this disease that eats away at the body, giving the average patient only two to five years to survive once detected. The future is not bleak in the treatment of this disease and progress is being made in the management of symptoms.

Epilogue

Surprisingly the voice that answered my "hello" was a dear friend and my former employer from Caddo Parish Sheriff's Office. Was I hearing right? I was being offered back the job I had just retired from the last day of December 2004. A few months short of one year, in September 2005 I was being asked to return.

Discussion climaxed to an unexpected end as I agreed to a part-time position. I can say no easily enough but God was calling me out of retirement, albeit a short-lived one and I knew I must answer His calling.

Employed once again, it has come as no surprise that the Lord wants me readily available to pray and minister to the deputies and their family members and friends. Oh, I have had a nice rest but will stay as long as I am needed or until God says it is time for retirement—again.

Exciting and miraculous things are still happening in my personal life as I continue to walk with the Lord and trust Him for my every need. It is my joy to share with you a major miracle—a much needed one—that has just recently happened.

The torrential rains and jagged lightning were sorely tempting me not to listen to the still, small voice quietly speaking to my heart. Showers of blessings would reward my braving the driving rain and gusting winds to obey the Voice. Donning an umbrella and raincoat served as little protection as I pressed through the storm into Wal Mart, very much against my will but not my better judgment, since I knew the silent, but definite, voice I was obeying was without question the voice of God.

As I made my way around the store, anticipation of why I was destined to be there that particularly stormy day brought a smile as rivulets of water continued dripping from previously dry apparel. Anticipation was about to meet head on with its counterpart—exhilarating joy. With "spiritual antennae" tuned in just right, I rolled the cart to a stop as I was being summoned by a gentleman near the pharmacy.

"How do you like the Humana Supplement for Medicare offered by the President?" he inquired.

Glad for an opportunity to voice an opinion, I took a seat and began talking. "I do not care for it at all. There are no benefits in it for me. One of my much needed medications, Rilutek, is not available on the program. At $850 per month I can no longer afford it no matter how much I need it."

The results Rilutek could offer may be worth such a ridiculously steep price, but that knowledge failed to increase my income a single penny. Although the medication does not cure ALS, it does slow the symptoms noticeably, and my digression had been notable since being forced to discontinue it one year earlier.

After listening attentively to my response, he asked, "Ma'am, do you have your medications filled at Wal Mart Pharmacy?"

"Yes, I do," I answered.

"Follow me." As I followed the beckoning man—who incidentally was the Representative for Humana—to the pharmacy, I could not help but wonder what exactly was going on here. This was too unusual to be anything other than the destination for which God had me push through the stormy weather.

Getting the pharmacist's attention, the representative began to explain my dilemma and obvious—and understandable—unhappiness with the new program. The pharmacist made his way to the computer and scanned for Rilutek. What a surprise! The price came up at $75 a month! Little did I know that this recent offer by our President would have such rewards after all. Victorious triumph filled my soul with joy. Satan is out to steal everything he can from God's children, even by trying to hide the truth behind vicious storm clouds. But he was busted by obedience to God's voice as his deceitful darkness was exposed by the Light.

Having been off Rilutek for one year had certainly made my appreciation of having it again overflow into thanksgiving and praise to God. Undoubtedly He had a reason for the year I had to go without it. God always has a reason for anything that happens in our lives.

Making inquiry of my other four medications proved the raging storm outside of no effect as well. Quite to the contrary, more "showers" fell as each one dropped from $15 to almost half at $8.50. God is so astonishing and faithful. No matter how mountainous a situation may seem, faith can move the mountain out of the way. This firm belief had not been proved wrong.

It goes without saying that faith and trust in God continues to be the overcoming factor in all of life's hurdles. Faith dictates that God made it possible to get the drug at a fraction of the previous cost, plus all others at barely over one-half the previous price. Calm assurance remains that if that was not possible, God is still in charge of every detail in my life. And who could argue the point after yet another miraculous feat accomplished by God alone.

Though the storms brew and the clouds swirl threateningly, the rays of hope and light are not prevented from slashing victoriously through the ominous clouds. The darkness of a stormy day does not dim the Light in the Valley. Jesus will shine forever, and I pray you will see His light in your valley so others can see that radiant light brightly projecting into their valleys to give them hope.

When I Met My Savior

I spent wasted years in useless pleasure.
Many hours I lived in idle play.
My heart was breaking,
I was restless and longing for a better way.
Then I met my sweet Savior.
On that day twilight dim
Joy filled my soul, defeat vanished and
Now I'm happy since Jesus' love came in.
****

Miss Mary

The Light in the Valley is available at amazon.com, the CreateSpace eStore and other retailers.

For the eBook version of *The Light in the Valley* visit the author's webpage at Smashwords.com.

Other eBooks available by author:
God's Glorious Symphony an expose' on Nature and God
Halloween: Hallowed or Heinous? an apologetic about the traditions
GhiAna's Jewels a fictional short story about Christmas
Rhythms of Love an array of poems about love in relationships

Mrs. Rachal welcomes your comments or questions at proofnedit@inbox.com. Visit her on Facebook and her blog at http://patrachal.blogspot.com/. To see Miss Mary's picture and an article about her go to the following address: http://www.als-mda.org/publications/als/als5_4.html#faith.

Thank you for reading our book and may the Lord bless you richly each day.

Made in the USA
Charleston, SC
27 October 2011